A Day with a Chef

By Hilary Dole Klein

The
Child's
World®
www.childsworld.com

Published in the United States of America by The Child's World®
1980 Lookout Drive • Mankato, MN 56003-1705
800-599-READ • www.childsworld.com

ACKNOWLEDGMENTS

The Child's World®: Mary Berendes, Publishing Director

Produced by Shoreline Publishing Group LLC
President / Editorial Director: James Buckley, Jr.
Designer: Tom Carling, carlingdesign.com
Cover Design: Slimfilms

Photo Credits
Cover—Dreamstime.com (main); Mike Eliason (insets)
Interior—All photos by Mike Eliason except: Dreamstime.com:
6, 29; Getty Images: 9; iStock: 8.

LIBRARY OF CONGRESS CATALOG-IN-PUBLICATION DATA

Klein, Hilary Dole, 1945–
 A day with a chef / By Hilary Dole Klein.
    p. cm. — (Reading rocks!)
 Includes index.
 ISBN 978-1-59296-857-2 (library bound : alk. paper)
 1. Cooks—Juvenile literature. I. Title. II. Series.

TX652.5.K58 2008
641.5092—dc22

                                        2007016849

CONTENTS

LET'S MEET
the Chef

Do you like to eat out? At restaurants, the person in charge of the kitchen is the chef (SHEF). A chef oversees everything that goes on in a restaurant and its kitchen.

Some chefs go to cooking school, while others learn on the job. Becoming a chef takes years of training and experience. A chef's hours are very long and the work can be hard. Being a chef means being very busy and having lots of responsibilities.

Chef Jason Banks is the **executive** chef at a busy restaurant called Fresco at the Beach in Santa Barbara, California. Not only is Jason the top person in the kitchen, but he's also responsible for the whole restaurant. Let's find out how he does his job.

The buttons on Jason's chef jacket are made of cloth. Plastic or metal buttons might melt while he works over a very hot stove!

5

One of Jason's first jobs was working at a grill restaurant, cooking food over a coal fire.

When Jason was growing up, he loved to watch his grandfather cook for family gatherings. He saw how great food made everyone happy. "Food brought our family together," he says.

Jason was in high school when he got his first kitchen job. After that, Jason always had a job cooking somewhere—in a **deli**, at a beachside cafe, or even in a family restaurant. Jason has washed dishes, peeled potatoes, made salads, and fried hamburgers. He's done just about everything a person can do in a kitchen!

"Deli" is short for "delicatessen," a type of food store that sells sandwiches and other handy items.

"The good thing about being a chef," says Jason, "is that you can get a job anywhere in the world." He has cooked in California, Washington, and Hawaii.

When Jason is not at his restaurant, he likes to surf and bodyboard, ride mountain bikes, and play beach volleyball. But what Jason likes best in the world is to "watch people enjoy the food I have prepared."

Catering companies often provide trays of food that serve lots of people.

When Jason was 22, he and his mother opened a **catering** business. This was like having a restaurant that changed buildings every day. One day, they served a small lunch at someone's home. The next day, they served 700 people in a tent.

Jason worked at the catering business for five years. To learn even more, Jason decided to go to cooking school. He studied "culinary arts" (the fancy name for cooking skills) in Portland, Oregon. Cooking school is like a regular school, with books to read and papers to write. But instead of sitting in a classroom, students also make food in a kitchen. Students learn cooking and baking skills. They study food safety. They learn how to run a restaurant, too.

While in cooking school, Jason was still working. To pay for school, he worked in a restaurant until long after midnight. Then he was up before dawn for classes. Jason was tired, but he got his **degree**.

A cooking teacher (tall hat) shows her students how to work on a piece of beef.

Part of the fun of eating at Jason's restaurant is enjoying the beautiful view of the Pacific Ocean.

After all that work and school, Jason finally got to open a restaurant. Fresco at the Beach opened in 2006, and Jason was there from the start. These days, he comes to work around noon and does not leave the restaurant until almost midnight. As the chef, he creates the recipes and plans the menus. He also orders all the food and supplies.

Plus, he's in charge of a big team of workers. And he has to do many of these things at the same time!

In addition to the restaurant's kitchen workers, Jason is in charge of the people who work "out front." That includes the **hosts**, the servers (waiters and waitresses), and the "runners" who bring the food to the tables. He even works with the people who clean the dishes.

"Going to a cooking school is a good way to get hired by a top restaurant," says Jason, "although you may still have to start out at the bottom washing dishes."

Since all restaurants need to attract customers, Jason also gives interviews to newspapers and magazines. Some chefs teach classes or appear on television shows. It's a busy life, but Jason says he's most comfortable in the kitchen.

A VERY Busy Day

Let's take a behind-the-scenes look at Jason's restaurant. When Jason arrives, his first job is to make sure that all the food for the day has arrived. He checks the foods' **quality**. Is the fish fresh? Are the strawberries firm and sweet? Are there enough pork chops?

If something is not perfect, Jason has new food delivered right away. He works with many companies that supply all the kinds of food the restaurant needs. Sometimes Jason visits one of the local farmers' markets. There he can see what fruits and vegetables are available. These visits give him ideas for his recipes.

While Jason (opposite page) makes sure the restaurant has all the food it needs, other staff members set the tables for the evening. They fold napkins and put out silverware.

Before Jason can cook any meals, he has to know how many people might be coming into the restaurant. The reservation book gives him the answers.

In the late afternoon, the restaurant is empty—but the staff is busy! Servers and other workers set the tables and polish glasses. They check candles and set out oil, vinegar, salt, and pepper.

Jason checks the **reservation** books to see how busy they will be that evening. He walks around and makes sure that everything is set up. In the kitchen, he checks the **prep** work. He visits the walk-in refrigerator to decide on the specials of the day.

"I never know what I will do until I see what we have and just think," he says. "Sometimes thinking is the most important part of this job."

A refrigerator full of food gives Jason ideas for new dishes to cook each night.

When Jason has decided on the dishes, he goes over them with the cooks. They make a sample of each dish. Everyone tastes them. It's important for everyone who works in the restaurant to know the food Jason will serve.

This prep cook is slicing calamari (squid!) for use in a tasty dish.

Hours before the hungry customers appear, the kitchen is already busy. The pastry chef makes desserts. He or she might bake apple tarts or chocolate cake.

Prep cooks trim chicken, clean shrimp, and chop vegetables. They also make soups, sauces, and salad dressings.

During the meal, the **line cooks** work the "line" where the food is cooked. They work on a stove with fiery burners. They cook on a grill, like a big barbecue. Line cooks have to remember lots of different orders. Line cooks might fry oysters, cook mushrooms, and grill fish all at the same time.

The **sous chef** (SOO SHEF) is the kitchen's second-in-command. This chef makes sure the specials are made exactly as Jason wants.

Jason is on top of it all. He decides what will be cooked, and in what order. He makes sure all the dishes are cooked properly, and that the plate looks good before it goes to the customer. And he makes sure everyone gets the right order!

"Sous" means "under" in French. Many cooking words come from that language.

Sous chef Brian puts sauces on a chicken dish at the start of the "line."

Dinner time! The restaurant is filling up. The servers take orders and put them into a computer. Jason calls out dinner orders to the cooks. "I need a roasted rack of lamb. I need **sautéed** mushrooms and grilled prawns. I need a rib-eye steak and a vegetable platter." To a salad maker he says: "Greens, no broccoli. Add goat cheese."

Jason watches as Brian puts a grilled chicken breast on top of potatoes and vegetables.

After the line cooks have prepared the plates, Jason checks them. Then he passes the meal to a runner who will carry it to the customer.

The line cooks dish up the food. Jason takes the plates and checks them. He wipes the edges of the plate to remove drips. He puts a piece of rosemary on the plate as a **garnish**. He's also watching all the other orders and tickets and cooks.

Jason may be the boss, but the restaurant really works as one giant team. "Everyone moves as if in a dance," he says. "We're so fast. We can do 180 meals in two hours."

Jason makes sure that a salad looks as good as it will taste.

As the evening slows down, Jason decides which workers can go home. On a slow night, he'll send people home and cook by himself. When all the diners have been fed, Jason goes into his office and orders food for the next day. Every day is a different order. Maybe everyone in the restaurant ordered chicken and no one ordered steak. That means Jason will need to order more chicken but no steak for the next night. Jason says that all the paperwork he has to do at night is the hardest part of his job.

Jason leaves for home around 10 or 11 at night. The sous chef is still at work, putting everything back in place. After making sure the floors are clean and the recycling and garbage are taken out, the dishwasher is the last person to go home.

Jason says the dishwasher is one of the most important people in the kitchen. "If the plate is dirty, it does not matter how good the food is. And if the dishwasher is out, we're in big trouble."

MAKING A GREAT Meal

Let's follow along with Jason as he prepares one special meal—we'll go from when it's ordered to when it's served.

A printer on the counter clicks out a ticket. Table 10 wants *coq au vin* (chicken in wine sauce) with smashed potatoes.

Knives

Knives are a chef's most important tools. Jason has 15! Chefs take very good care of their knives, which can be very expensive. Most chefs don't let anyone touch their knives, even the sous chef.

Jason calls out the order and the line cooks get busy. All the pieces of the meal come together quickly.

Earlier in the day, the prep cooks washed, peeled, and boiled big pots of potatoes. They also cut and trimmed dozens of chickens. Other cooks have chopped and diced carrots, onions, and mushrooms. (Good chefs can chop, shred, or slice vegetables in dozens of ways.)

OPPOSITE PAGE
Computers in the kitchen? The servers use a computer to send orders from the restaurant's "front" to the kitchen. Jason and his staff use the printed tickets to keep track of the orders.

To keep the vegetables from burning, Jason shakes the pan and flips the veggies up in the air.

Jason will cook this order himself. He starts with the chicken. He coats a pan with olive oil and adds cut-up chicken. He **browns** the chicken until it's a golden color. Then he removes the chicken from the pan and sets it aside. Next, he browns some bacon in the empty pan.

Then Jason adds chopped onions, carrots, and mushrooms. He pours in some red wine, some white wine, and some brandy. He stirs and scrapes the pan, getting little bits of chicken and bacon into the sauce. Then Jason lights a match and POOF—the sauce is on fire! This gives the sauce more flavor. The fire burns out, and Jason adds the chicken he set aside earlier. He adds some salt and pepper.

This flame doesn't burn the food. Instead, it gives the sauce more flavor.

Time to check the potatoes. After cooking in this big pot, they'll be "smashed" before being served.

Now Jason makes the potatoes to go with the chicken. In a small pan, butter and cream are warmed together. This mixture is poured over the potatoes, which are in another pan. Next comes the fun part—Jason smashes everything together with a big spoon!

Normally, another cook would dish the potatoes and chicken onto a plate and hand it over to Jason. Jason checks the plate carefully. He wipes the edges with a cloth and adds a garnish. Then a runner carries it to the hungry customer.

The meal is done! Now it's time to make dozens more. Jason grabs a ticket and gets to work. He's always busy, but he's happy. He's doing what he loves best: cooking!

Ta-dah! This is what coq au vin *looks like when it's finished. The browned chicken is placed atop the vegetables and potatoes. The green rosemary leaves are the garnish.*

GET
Cookin'!

Here's an easy recipe from Jason for frosted cupcakes that you can make with your family.

Vanilla Cupcakes

3 cups cake flour
2 cups sugar
2½ teaspoons baking powder
½ teaspoon salt
1 cup butter (2 sticks)
1 cup milk
4 eggs
2 teaspoons vanilla

Ask an adult to preheat the oven to 350°. In a big bowl, mix together the flour, sugar, baking powder, and salt. One by one, add the butter, milk, eggs, and vanilla. Mix everything well. Spoon the mixture into cupcake pans lined with paper cups. Bake for 10 minutes, or until a toothpick inserted in the middle comes out clean.

Chocolate Buttercream Frosting

¼ cup cocoa powder
¾ cup powdered sugar
½ cup softened butter

In a bowl, mix these things together well. You can do this with a spoon and lots of muscle, or get help with an electric hand mixer.

When the cupcakes are cool, take them out of the pan. Use a knife to spread the frosting on top.

Now you're on your way to becoming a chef!

GLOSSARY

browns cooks the outside of the food lightly

catering delivering or preparing food for a party or event

degree what a student earns for finishing college or other higher school

deli a small restaurant that serves sandwiches, meats, and cheeses

executive a person in charge of other workers

garnish greens, fruits, or flowers added to a finished dish to make it look nicer

hosts restaurant workers who take customers to the tables

line cooks kitchen workers who prepare plates of food

prep short for prepare; to get ready

quality in food, a state of being good to eat

reservation when a table is held for a customer or group who will come in later

sautéed lightly fried in a pan

sous chef the second-in-command of a kitchen

FIND OUT MORE

BOOKS

The Best Chef in Second Grade
by Katherine Kenah (Harper Collins, 2007)
A novel for kids about a girl who really, really loves to cook.

Emeril! There's a Chef in My Soup!
by Emeril Lagasse (Harper Collins, 2005)
A famous TV chef gives cooking tips and recipes for kids.

I Want to Be a Chef
by Stephanie Maze (Harcourt Brace, 1999)
Learn the steps to take if you want to make cooking your career.

WEB SITES

Visit our Web page for lots of links about chefs and cooking:
www.childsworld.com/links

Note to Parents, Teachers, and Librarians: We routinely check our Web links to make sure they're safe, active sites—so encourage your readers to check them out!

INDEX

HILARY DOLE KLEIN is a writer and editor living in Santa Barbara, California. She has written hundreds of articles on topics ranging from ant invasions to rock 'n' roll. For a few years, as a restaurant critic for the *Los Angeles Times* and other newspapers, Hilary had to eat for a living! She first met Chef Jason when she interviewed him for a magazine article.